92

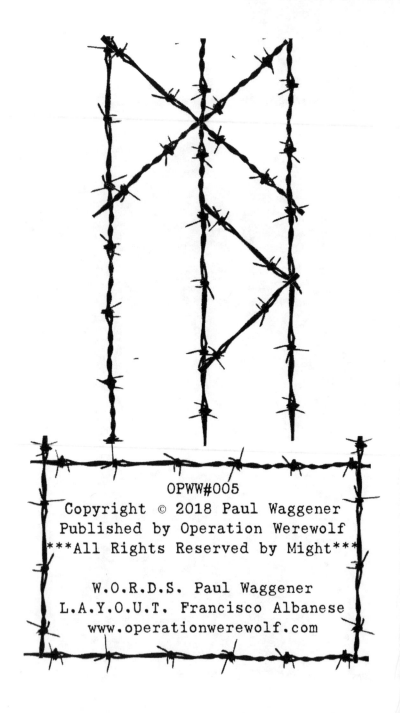

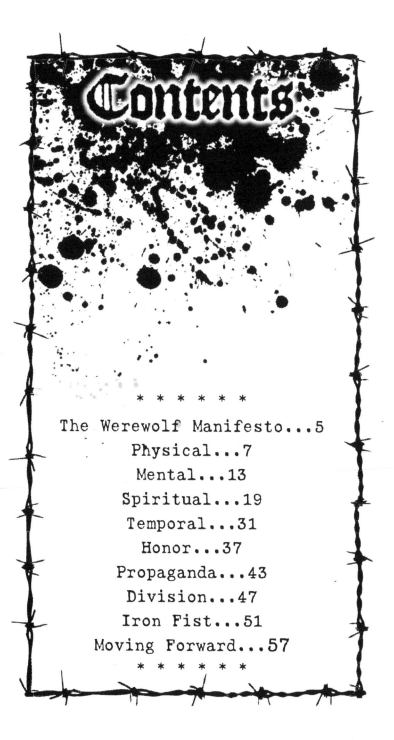

Contents

* * * * * *

The Werewolf Manifesto...5

Physical...7

Mental...13

Spiritual...19

Temporal...31

Honor...37

Propaganda...43

Division...47

Iron Fist...51

Moving Forward...57

* * * * * *

IRON & BlOOD.

THE WEREWOLF MANIFESTO

W.A.R.

At the time of this writing, Operation Werewolf is heading into its 6th year of existence. What began as a phrase written on the cover of one man's training journal has grown into a philosophy, and from there, into a worldwide movement.

Because of this vital, unstoppable expansion, it has become necessary to release this manifesto as a clarification of intent--there should be no uncertainty as to our aims and goals, and they are not secret.

In this brief, sharp manuscript, I have outlined what I consider to be the core concepts of Operation Werewolf, and stated them in the clearest way I know how. It should act as both a beacon fire for the strong and a deterrent to the tourist and the insincere, as there is no other way to interpret what we do outside of these words.

My own writing up to this point has been largely in the form of essays and smaller pieces of interconnected writing that creates a sort of circuitry which signals back to a core that has as yet been unstated.

I will do my best to avoid redundancy, and this book is not a restructuring of anything that has gone before, but will act instead as a reinforcement, and as a basic blueprint of sorts- a map that outlines the concept of Total Life Reform and gives one a compass to begin their own navigation.

--Paul Waggener, Winter 2018.
Oregon Coast.

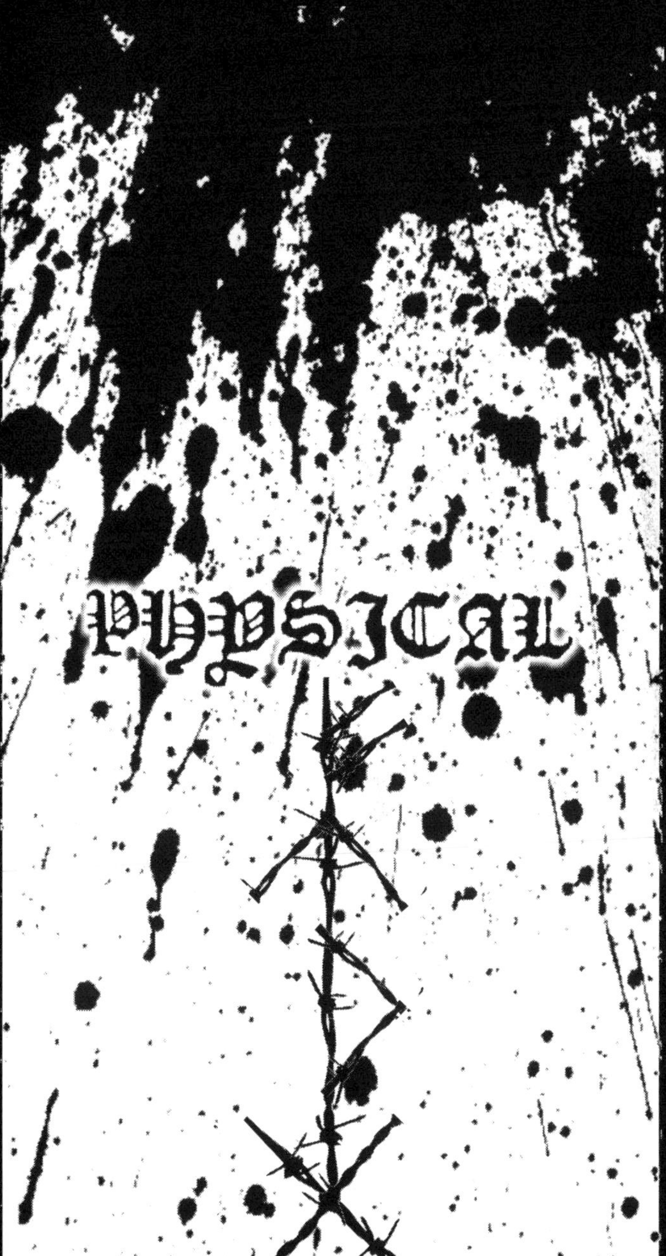
PHYSICAL

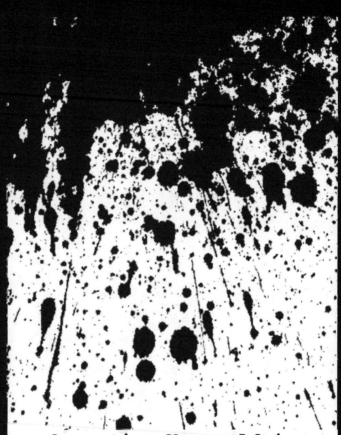

Operation Werewolf is a physical culture.

We have used the term "Militant Strength Culture" in the past, and have done so without an intention of irony, as in all things. We have a sense of humor, and love to laugh, but we are not ironic. Irony is the last bastion of the weakest men- never having to stand for anything, never having to display or develop conviction.

What we mean by Militant Strength Culture can be summed up simply in looking at the words that make up the phrase.

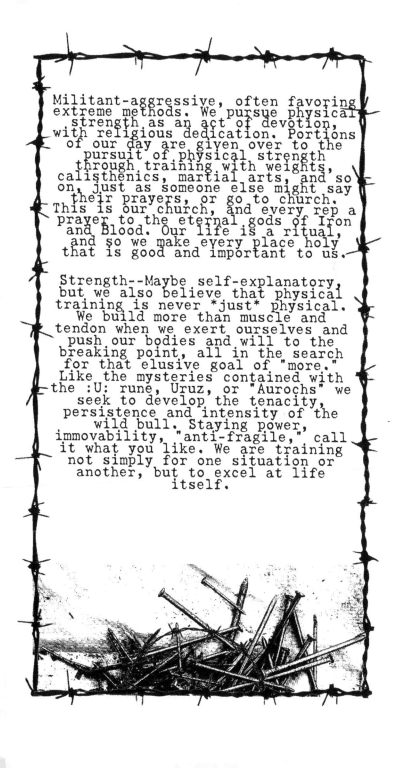

Militant-aggressive, often favoring extreme methods. We pursue physical strength as an act of devotion, with religious dedication. Portions of our day are given over to the pursuit of physical strength through training with weights, calisthenics, martial arts, and so on, just as someone else might say their prayers, or go to church. This is our church, and every rep a prayer to the eternal gods of Iron and Blood. Our life is a ritual, and so we make every place holy that is good and important to us.

Strength--Maybe self-explanatory, but we also believe that physical training is never *just* physical. We build more than muscle and tendon when we exert ourselves and push our bodies and will to the breaking point, all in the search for that elusive goal of "more." Like the mysteries contained with the :U: rune, Uruz, or "Aurochs" we seek to develop the tenacity, persistence and intensity of the wild bull. Staying power, immovability, "anti-fragile," call it what you like. We are training not simply for one situation or another, but to excel at life itself.

Culture--One of the dictionary definitions of culture is "the customs, arts, social institutions, and achievements of a particular nation, people, or other social group." This is an accurate depiction of what we mean when we say we are creating a culture with Operation Werewolf. One that is worldwide, yet consistent. What does it look like, what is created from it, what has been achieved by those within it? If we are militantly strong, then we will be known by our works. If we are fragile, frail, ignorant, weak--the same.

Our culture will grow into a self-correcting environment dedicated to pressure, accountability, loyalty, honesty, ownership and responsibility, and creative spirit. It will reward and encourage strength and strong action, and it will discourage and revile weakness and weak actions from those who would wrongly attempt to wear the mantle as interlopers.

Because of this, we believe that physicality is completely irremovable from the core of Operation Werewolf. If you do not train for physical strength and mastery, and if you are not constantly and markedly improving, you cannot call yourself a part of what we do.

But if you are training, even if you have just begun your journey to physical and overall strength, and you are giving it your all, in a heroic effort, no matter how untrained and untried--then you are succeeding.

Remember that, before you compare yourself to the work of others: each journey begins when our hands meet the bar, the kettlebell, the glove or wrap, or we put on the gi. But we are all walking the same path, toward self-improvement and the chasing of legend. We cannot do so weak and unfit.

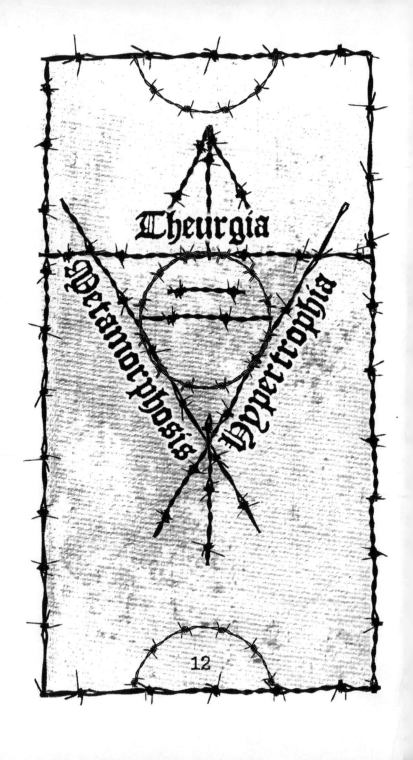

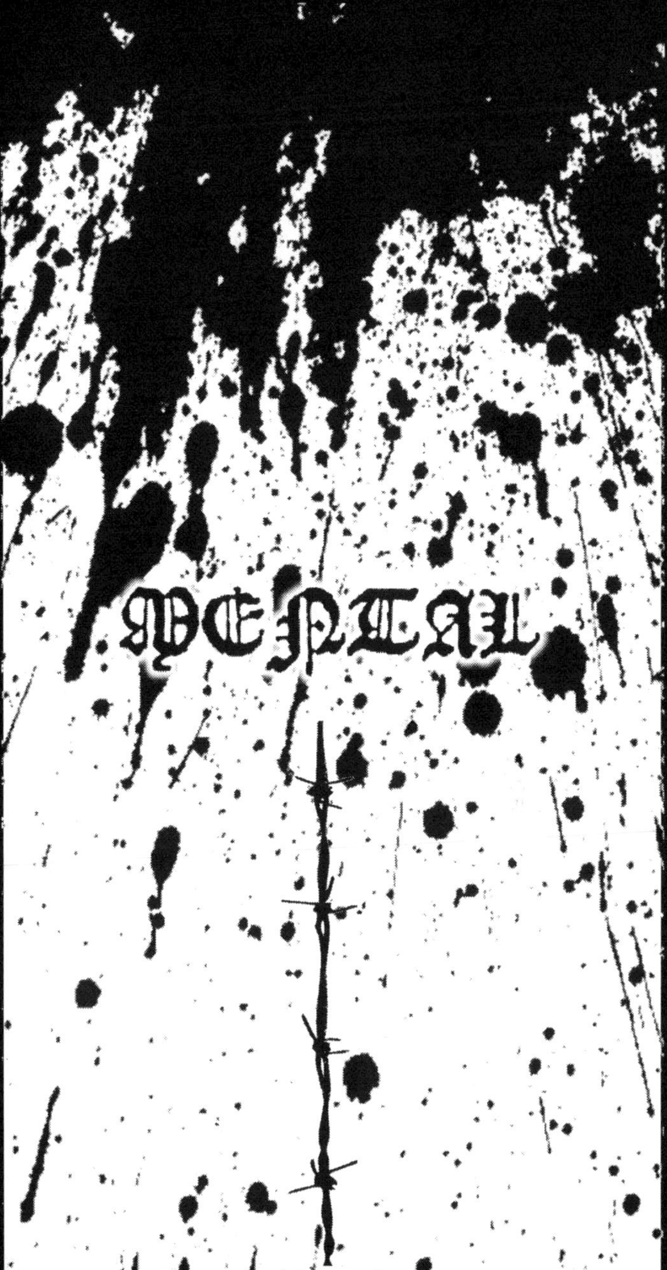
MENTAL

Strength is not simply relegated to
a base physical attribute.
Certainly, that is one quantifiable
area of strength, but it does not
contain the entirety of the idea.

We must develop mental strength
also, and in much the same way as
we train the body: through the
continuous, consistent, and correct
application of resistance and right
action. This looks different for
different areas of approach, but as
we stated in the previous section,
physical training is never just
physical. Those tortuous and trying
early mornings or late nights,
going to work out, to hit the track
or the training mats, putting
yourself through immense stresses,
and creating habit and skill--they
begin to develop a mental strength
and toughness as well.

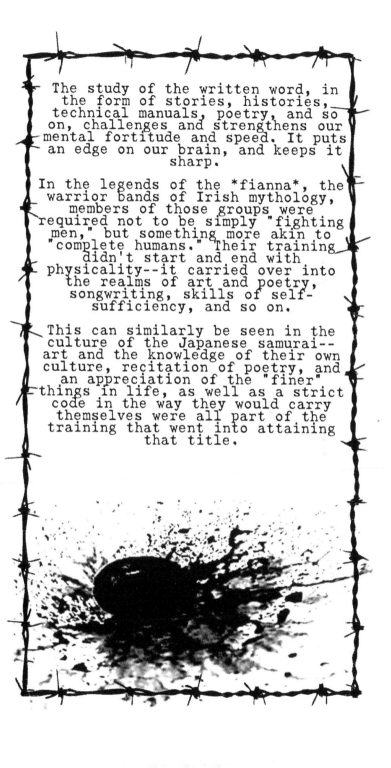

The study of the written word, in the form of stories, histories, technical manuals, poetry, and so on, challenges and strengthens our mental fortitude and speed. It puts an edge on our brain, and keeps it sharp.

In the legends of the *fianna*, the warrior bands of Irish mythology, members of those groups were required not to be simply "fighting men," but something more akin to "complete humans." Their training didn't start and end with physicality--it carried over into the realms of art and poetry, songwriting, skills of self-sufficiency, and so on.

This can similarly be seen in the culture of the Japanese samurai-- art and the knowledge of their own culture, recitation of poetry, and an appreciation of the "finer" things in life, as well as a strict code in the way they would carry themselves were all part of the training that went into attaining that title.

When we think of our own training,
we should apply this attention to
"completeness." Instead of our
training breaking down into only
sets, reps, or hours on the track
or the mat, we should go deeper.
Demand more of ourselves. Why apply
this kind of attention and
organization only to our physical
training? We should be programming
our reading time, "getting those
pages in," putting in work
identifying and rooting out
negative characteristics through
time given over to meditation and
self-knowledge. Studying business
and finance in order to attain
self-sufficiency and temporal
power, so that our family or tribe
can have more personal freedom, and
leverage in this world.

Language too, the history of our
own people's culture, and that of
others, human psychology and
mythology, to round out our
understanding of the framework
within which we exist, and must
thrive.

Memorization and recitation of texts that we find strengthening, beautiful or inspiring. Studies show that memorization of mantra or verse has a positive impact on the brain- how strange, that exercise should be good for the mind in the same way that it is good for the body! These ideas are obvious, but often go unpracticed, and those who look only to grow and improve in one area will find those others to languish, and atrophy.

Gaining an appreciation for art and culture is not some empty, bourgeois act or bid to become some kind of *intelligentsia*. It grows and deepens our knowledge of, and therefore, power within, the entire structure of humanity and its history on the planet. Music, language, art, poetry--these are all tongues, and keys of unlocking the secrets of the universe as surely as mathematics.

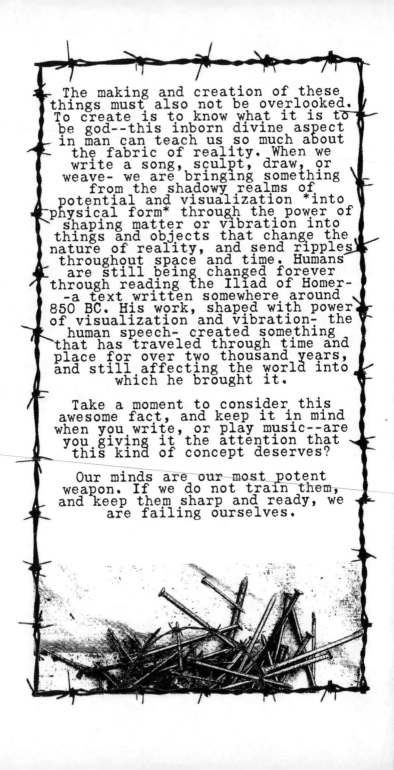

The making and creation of these
things must also not be overlooked.
To create is to know what it is to
be god--this inborn divine aspect
in man can teach us so much about
the fabric of reality. When we
write a song, sculpt, draw, or
weave- we are bringing something
from the shadowy realms of
potential and visualization *into
physical form* through the power of
shaping matter or vibration into
things and objects that change the
nature of reality, and send ripples
throughout space and time. Humans
are still being changed forever
through reading the Iliad of Homer-
-a text written somewhere around
850 BC. His work, shaped with power
of visualization and vibration- the
human speech- created something
that has traveled through time and
place for over two thousand years,
and still affecting the world into
which he brought it.

Take a moment to consider this
awesome fact, and keep it in mind
when you write, or play music--are
you giving it the attention that
this kind of concept deserves?

Our minds are our most potent
weapon. If we do not train them,
and keep them sharp and ready, we
are failing ourselves.

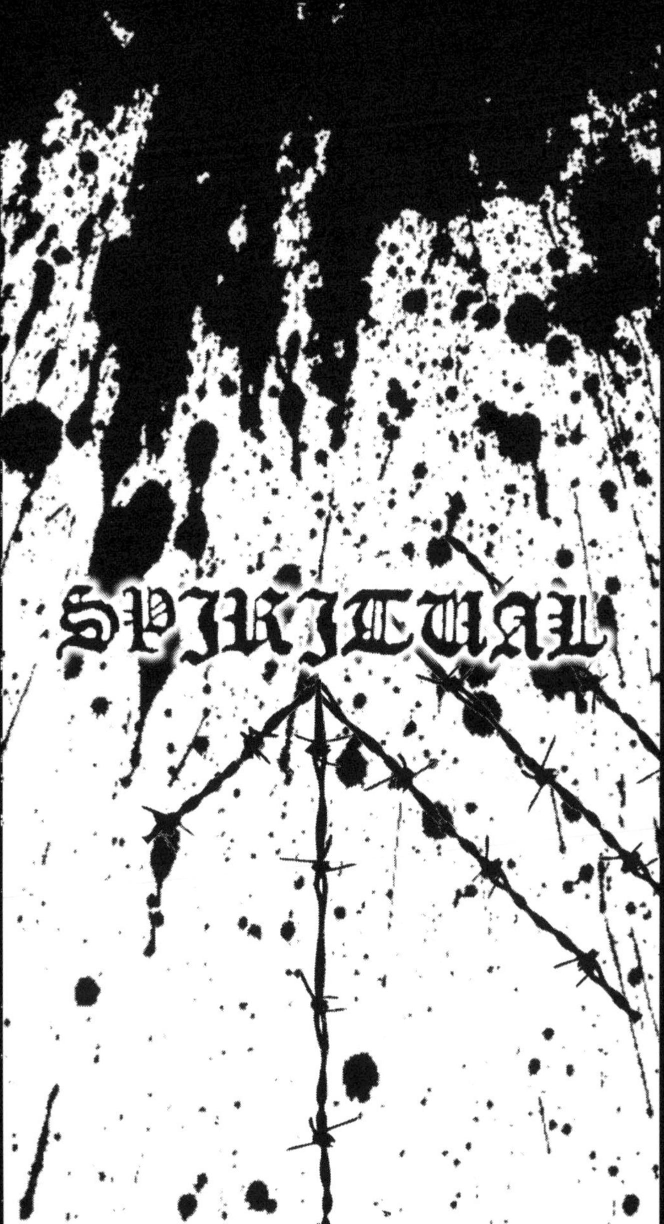
SPIRITUAL

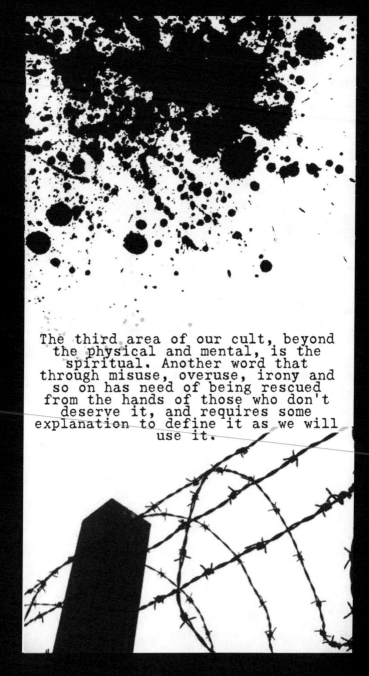

The third area of our cult, beyond the physical and mental, is the spiritual. Another word that through misuse, overuse, irony and so on has need of being rescued from the hands of those who don't deserve it, and requires some explanation to define it as we will use it.

In its simplest terms, when we use this word, we will be referring to the intangible thing within man which can be seen as the seat of his character, emotions, and connection with the unseen world around him. Also, his will, and other such unquantifiable concepts that man has felt, interacted with, and experienced, knows to be real, but cannot show in a physical form--but certainly can see the effects of.

Just as we cannot see "love" as anything beyond an assortment of chemicals in the brain, but can witness it in a mother's devotion to her son, or a man's to his wife; just as we cannot see "will" as chemical combination or a physical form, we can witness it in the determination of a mountain climber, a monk setting his body on fire, or even someone resisting the addiction of cigarettes or narcotics--we cannot see the "soul" or "spirit" of a man, or his "character," but we can see the change they create in the world about him.

This concept often causes resistance from human beings in our present time, our present place in history and its wider culture.

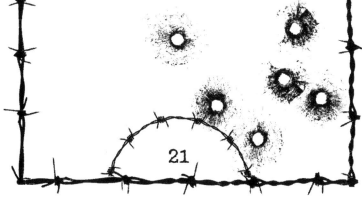

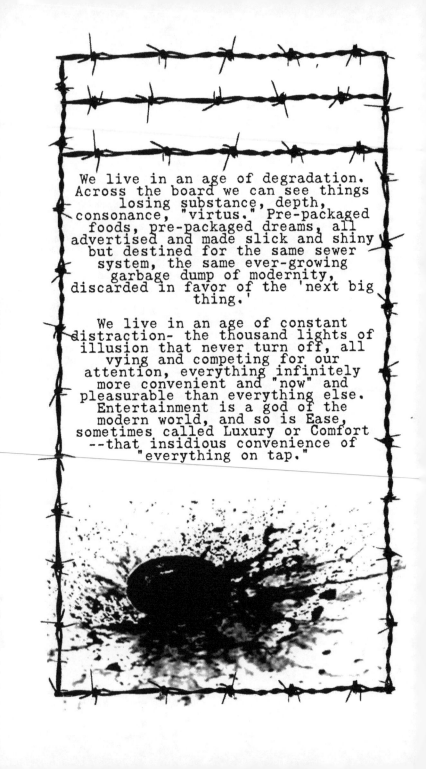

We live in an age of degradation.
Across the board we can see things
losing substance, depth,
consonance, "virtus." Pre-packaged
foods, pre-packaged dreams, all
advertised and made slick and shiny
but destined for the same sewer
system, the same ever-growing
garbage dump of modernity,
discarded in favor of the 'next big
thing.'

We live in an age of constant
distraction- the thousand lights of
illusion that never turn off, all
vying and competing for our
attention, everything infinitely
more convenient and "now" and
pleasurable than everything else.
Entertainment is a god of the
modern world, and so is Ease,
sometimes called Luxury or Comfort
--that insidious convenience of
"everything on tap."

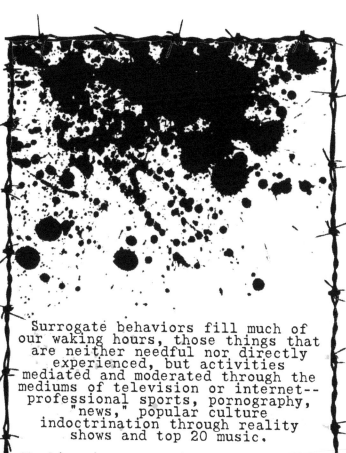

Surrogate behaviors fill much of
our waking hours, those things that
are neither needful nor directly
experienced, but activities
mediated and moderated through the
mediums of television or internet--
professional sports, pornography,
"news," popular culture
indoctrination through reality
shows and top 20 music.

We live in an age in which meaning
or belief has not simply been lost,
but one in which it is rejected
outright. Believing in something is
'out of style,' something for
fanatics, madmen, outcasts and
pariahs from the towering glass
structures of the world shopping
mall, these great cathedrals of the
new pilgrimage. Belief is
inconvenient, unpopular, decidedly
uncool unless ironic or "for now,"
ugly, dirty, not politically
correct, and possibly even some
kind of -ist or -ism. It is looked
on with suspicion, distaste, and
often times fear and anger.

I am telling you, we must be these
fanatics and madmen. We must wear
the mantle of the outcast, the
outlaw and pariah, and we must do
so with terrible joy. We must live
lives of inconvenient conviction,
unpopular to the mass of shoppers
and consumers, reinforcers of
illusion, merchants of false hope
and dreams. Not ironic, but
sincere, with a fearless laughter
born of bold humor and clear vision
that strikes deep at the heart of
their lie.

We will be hated--but only by those
who have been conditioned to hate,
and by those who have done the
conditioning. By strong men and
women, and spiritual outlaws, and
wanderers at the border, defiant
ones and rebels, we will be loved.
And we will be loved with a fury
and ferocity that is a conquering
force, invincible and holy as the
smoke of our sacrificial fires
rising to the heavens.

We must be possessed of a towering
and thunderous belief, a great red
ocean, a roaring, fiery, zealous
belief, unshakeable, violent as a
storm in the desert--and this
belief will be in meaning itself.
What we hunger and thirst for is
meaning. We want to know that ours
was a life lived for something, a
greater truth, something more than
the sum of its parts. We long for

tribe, strong connections with our
peer group and families, by blood
or oath. We crave a spiritual
framework to sink our roots into,
that grows through every facet of
our lives and enriches it, and us.
Because of these desires, we
shackle ourselves to the awe-full
responsibility of creation.

Like Odin and his brothers,
representations of consciousness
and ecstasy and will, fashioning
the world out of the raw materials
of potential and symbolism, or Lord
Shiva performing *tāṇḍavam*, the
divine dance that represents the
sacred act of the creative and
destructive cycle, we must take it
upon ourselves to build this
framework.

Our task is a holy one--the
holiest! Because we are the men at
the end of this iron age, this Kali
Yuga, who must rediscover the
connections with divinity, and in
drinking this ambrosia in the dark
and hidden places of the world, we
must carry it with us, like a torch
in the blackness. Our eyes must see
things unknown to the mundane, and
we must be initiated by wild holy
men at great fires held at
sacrificial feasts in the woods, so
that we can initiate others
desirous of this way we walk.

We must perform rituals daily, of
austerity and self-discipline,
because it is hard, and will make
us so in turn- this holy task
cannot be carried out by the weak
in spirit, nor the frail in body.
It calls for complete humans, who
seek and attain strength in all
realms of this existence--mental,
physical, spiritual, temporal.
These disciplines come in the form
of exercising the mind and body
through memorization, recitation,
singing, writing, lifting, running,
fighting and more. The attainment
of temporal strength by seeing it
as a simple game of dice, leverage
to be gained as one might in a
board game, so that he no longer
has to worry about or be confined
by the rules of the game, but plays
it his own way.

But we must also perform the
greater rituals, those that speak
to us in a deep resonation with the
ancient, as well as the present and
future. Rituals of fire and blood,
of wildness and divine madness.
Rituals of oath, and loyalty, honor
and tribal passage. These great
rites reinforce and empower our
daily ones, as each thing begins to
be seen as part of something
greater, and the monthly rituals
feed the yearly ones, which in turn

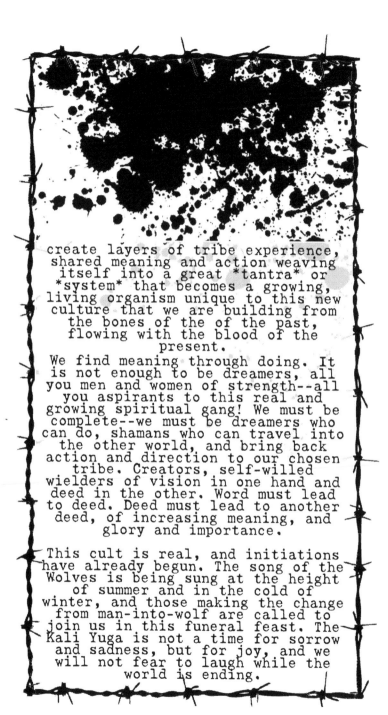

create layers of tribe experience,
shared meaning and action weaving
itself into a great *tantra* or
system that becomes a growing,
living organism unique to this new
culture that we are building from
the bones of the of the past,
flowing with the blood of the
present.

We find meaning through doing. It
is not enough to be dreamers, all
you men and women of strength--all
you aspirants to this real and
growing spiritual gang! We must be
complete--we must be dreamers who
can do, shamans who can travel into
the other world, and bring back
action and direction to our chosen
tribe. Creators, self-willed
wielders of vision in one hand and
deed in the other. Word must lead
to deed. Deed must lead to another
deed, of increasing meaning, and
glory and importance.

This cult is real, and initiations
have already begun. The song of the
Wolves is being sung at the height
of summer and in the cold of
winter, and those making the change
from man-into-wolf are called to
join us in this funeral feast. The
Kali Yuga is not a time for sorrow
and sadness, but for joy, and we
will not fear to laugh while the
world is ending.

Transform
from a man
into an arsenal
of mythic action

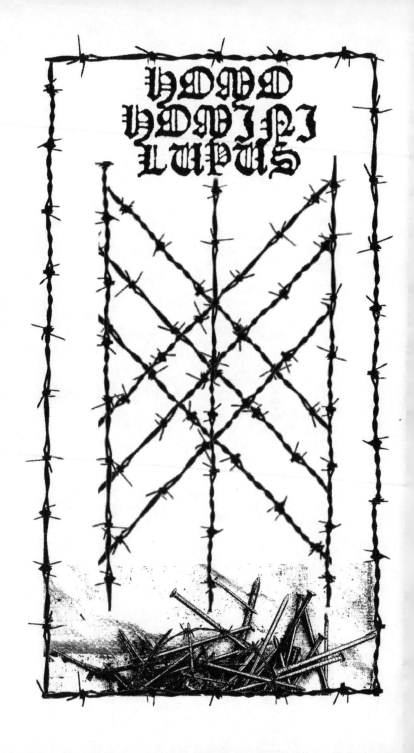

HOMO
HOMINI
LUPUS

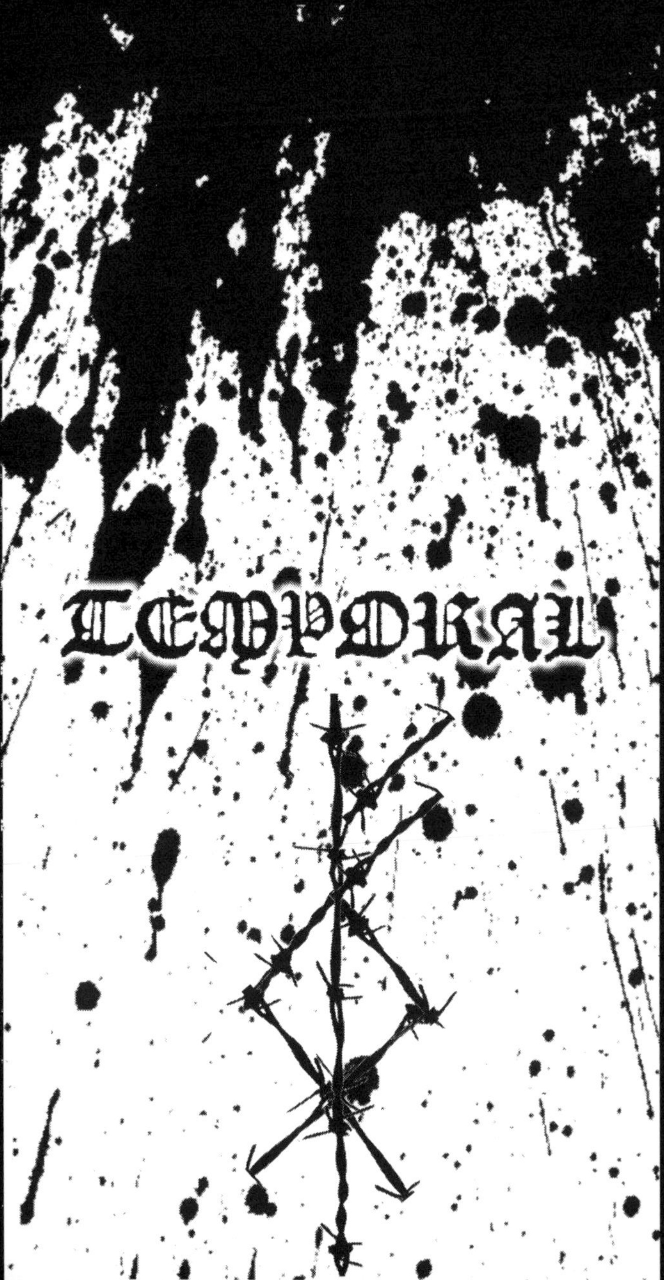
TEMPORAL

We can only live the way that we
have the resources to live. The
game in which we are playing has
set rules, and these rules,
although they can be bent and
sometimes broken, are also easily
leveraged simply by understanding
them enough to make them work for
you.

Making money, building networks and
acquiring resources can seem
esoteric, difficult, a special or
secret "trick" that some have and
some don't, but this is incorrect.
There are strategies--tested and
true ways to simply play the game
from a sound perspective, and
develop the basic skills required
to increase your personal resource
and wealth.

In the ancient Germanic tribal
system, a ruler was a ruler because
he could be--not only through
strength of arm, but of the wealth
amassed from his conquest. He
remained a ruler based on many
things, but high among them: his
ability to be generous. His ability
to "take care" of those who were
close to him, or important to him-
his most deadly warriors and
trusted allies.

There is a line between the
amassing of personal wealth as a
powerful means to an end, and an
obsession with money itself- but
too much time has been spent by
otherwise strong and intelligent
individuals on eschewing wealth as
some kind of "dirty" thing.

This self-willed poverty is largely
a Christian virtue, the denying of
possessions or material gain in
favor of some spiritual reward.

In this world, we must use the
currency of the world to attain our
goals, viewing it as a fuel source
which we burn to feed the greater
crusade, our holy mission, whatever
that may be. If we have big dreams
of travel, conquest, training,
owning land, building our tribal
infrastructure--we must use the
lifeblood of the time we live in to
attain these things. That lifeblood
is green, and gold.

Denying it is to deny the power of a hurricane, or an earthquake. The world does not require your tacit approval to be the way it is, it just is.

We can either bemoan our lot in life, beaten down by the day to day problems of rent, bills, "never enough," or "if I only had the money," or we can put our heads down and of the work. Put in the reps, the time spent on studying the form, the correct application of force, the modes of being and seeming, all the different hides we must wear. Treat it the same as you would any other form of your training: if you do the work and apply the correct expenditure of force against increasing resistance, you will achieve results.

In the current era in the Western world, it is easier than ever for anyone to utilize incredibly powerful technologies in order to learn, create, advertise and market any idea they can come up with. From the blacksmith to the cryptocurrency trader, old-world craftsman to dystopian free marketeer, anything imaginable can be turned into a business capable of sustaining the individual and his clan.

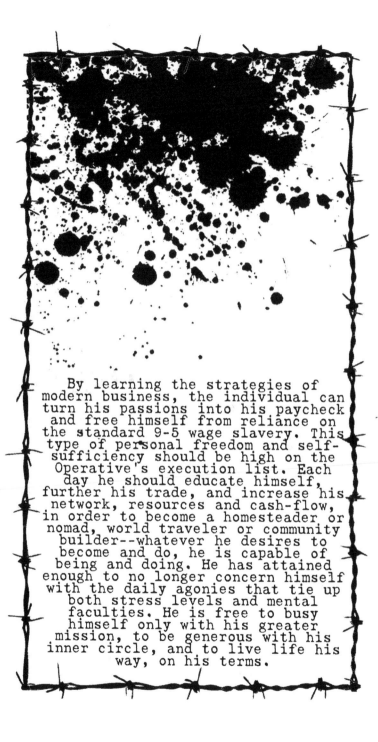

By learning the strategies of
modern business, the individual can
turn his passions into his paycheck
and free himself from reliance on
the standard 9-5 wage slavery. This
type of personal freedom and self-
sufficiency should be high on the
Operative's execution list. Each
day he should educate himself,
further his trade, and increase his
network, resources and cash-flow,
in order to become a homesteader or
nomad, world traveler or community
builder--whatever he desires to
become and do, he is capable of
being and doing. He has attained
enough to no longer concern himself
with the daily agonies that tie up
both stress levels and mental
faculties. He is free to busy
himself only with his greater
mission, to be generous with his
inner circle, and to live life his
way, on his terms.

Alchemical
Lycanthropy

HONOR

Honor, in brief, is the performance of actions that bring strength and enhanced reputation to the individual or peer group, and the adherence to a code of conduct set forth by the individual or the individual's peer group. Honor can certainly be cultivated alone, but this requires an incredibly clear and focused internal compass that holds the pre-requisite of the kind of self-awareness and merciless evaluation that most simply do not have, or have not attained.

Mostly, honor is about respect-- both the attainment of it through action, and the maintaining of it through consistent adherence to the "honor code" of the group a man has chosen as his peer group. Honor, because of this, is almost entirely dependent on that specific group's understanding of the term. Because of this, the word can never be used "universally." What is honorable to one peer group may be the height of flagrant dishonor to another.

Because of this, our conception and use of this term is always highly specialized and should never be applied to those outside of our immediate peer group to attempt "leverage." We cannot appeal to someone's sense of honor, when they have either no developed understanding of the word itself, or their definition disagrees with ours. If you'd like to see this in action, go ask five different people at random to define what the word means. You are likely to be met with confused explanations or incredibly vague ideas about moral structure, which leads us back the issue that morality is not universal either--what is "right" or "wrong" to us may have very little in common with what is right or wrong to someone from a foreign culture with a different upbringing and worldview than our own. Within the peer group, we must have a clearly established code of conduct, and this is our "honor code." With this honor code, we can maintain our group's integrity, reputation, and mutual respect, and we can use it to reinforce or to correct individuals who are slipping. In our modern age, we hear the word "shaming" used to denote a horrible thing that people can do to one another, from "slut-shaming" to "fat-shaming" or whatever other ridiculous term they are using now. But shame has always been used as an effective and powerful tool among men to enforce an honor code- if someone is failing, he is shamed into right action, and if this shaming fails, violence or expulsion might follow, or sometimes both.

But shame has always been used as
an effective and powerful tool
among men to enforce an honor code-
if someone is failing, he is shamed
into right action, and if this
shaming fails, violence or
expulsion might follow, or
sometimes both.

When an individual breaks the honor
code of his peer group, he is
saying with his actions that the
group is less important than his
immediate desires or choices- this
is an act of flagrant dishonor, and
must be corrected immediately by
the honor group, or it will spread
throughout the group like a cancer
until it becomes the social norm,
and the entire bedrock of the group
is eroded and corrupt. This is why
confrontation and accountability
within the group are key concepts
that must be reinforced always and
often- if there is no
confrontation, there is no
accountability. If no
accountability, there is no reason
to adhere to the code, if no
adherence, no group. It is our code
of conduct that draws the line
between "inside" and "outside,"
because at day's end, it is
orthopraxy, not orthodoxy that
separates us from outsiders. Not
what we say we believe, but what we
show the world with our actions.

This is the reason that Operation Werewolf must defend itself from interlopers. Our code of conduct is based on the following simple phrase:

"Strong Limbs. Pure Hearts. Actions Matching Words."

This breaks down into its three parts thusly:
The constant and consistent development of physical and mental strength, as outlined previously, but more than just that, a fanatical devotion to it. If we are not training as a religious act of zeal, we are bringing flagrant dishonor to the group--our immediate Division, Tribe, Gang, or peer group, but also to everyone associated with Operation Werewolf who lives by its tenets. If someone is never improving, chronically mediocre, never fully invested in their physical training or mental sharpening, they are in a state of dishonor and dishonesty.

Pure hearts could be taken in many ways, but what is meant when we use it is a victory over compulsive actions through successfully battling weakness, addiction, unhealthy and toxic behaviors and relationships, and the cessation of negative habits. This requires the development of a razor sharp self-awareness, a merciless inward gaze, a clinical eye toward our own weaknesses and failures, and an iron-hard dedication to their eradication. Individuals who are addicted to chemical substances, including the addiction to compulsive behaviors, that is, any action performed against one's conscious will due to uncontrolled impulse, are in a state of dishonor and dishonesty.

Actions matching words means that, as stated before, orthopraxy is always our highest goal, and that proper belief will come organically through correct, right action. We do what we say. We are what we do. We do what we know to be correct through an honest evaluation of ourselves that never ceases. This does not mean that anyone who makes mistakes or experiences failure over the course of their mission is dishonorable--defeat only comes through surrender. We all fail. We all engage in compulsive behaviors, and are susceptible to weakness and wrong action- it is only when we surrender to it and give up the fight that we are existing in a state of dishonesty and dishonor.

This battle is ongoing, and will last our entire lives. It is made up of countless objectives and missions, trials and ordeals, and the tactics used are myriad. It is fought in every word, in every deed, hardship, and experience we will ever undergo. We call this battle of overcoming Operation Werewolf.

PROPAGANDA

Operation Werewolf spreads its
message of strength and improvement
throughout the world through the
use of several different layers of
propaganda. We understand that to
the uninitiated this can become
confusing. We recommend that
individuals learn about Operation
Werewolf in the following ways,
listed by order of importance:

--Official Printed Works

At the time of this writing, The Werewolf Manifesto, the Complete Transmissions Volumes 1 and 2, and the Complete Zines are considered "foundational texts." They should be read by anyone affiliated.

--Inner Circle

The Inner Circle is a monthly communique in the form of a collection of videos and essays. The information disseminated there is specifically for "active Operatives" and those who are interested in a higher level of involvement and content. It can be found at our official website.

--War Journal and Video

The War Journal is where our public articles and essays are shared. It can be found on our website. All public videos can be found on YouTube by either searching for Operation Werewolf or going to Paul Waggener's channel.

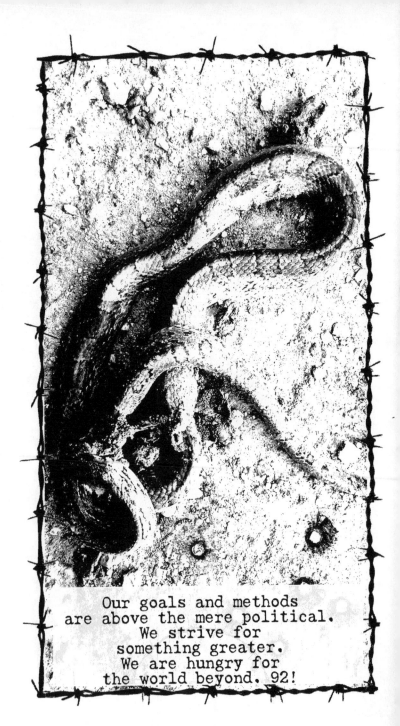

Our goals and methods
are above the mere political.
We strive for
something greater.
We are hungry for
the world beyond. 92!

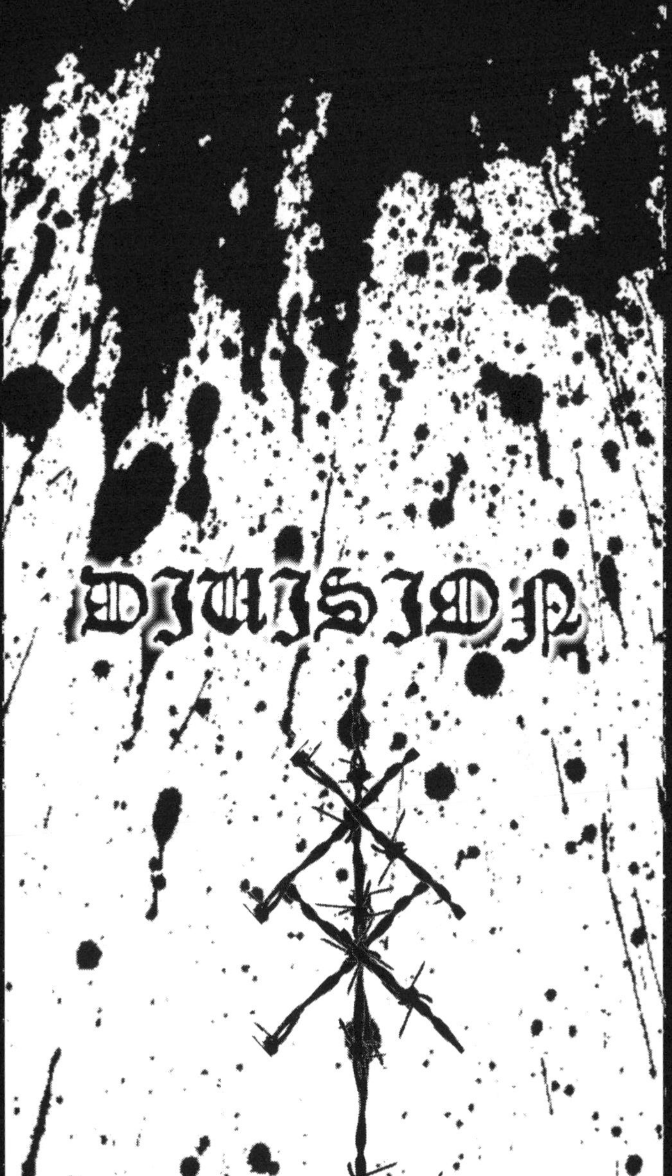
DIVISION

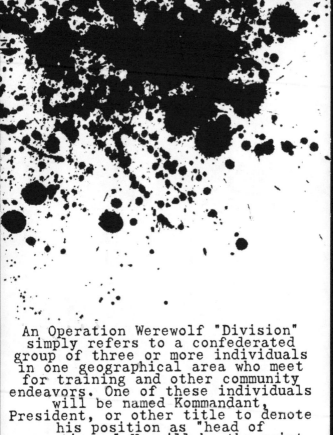

An Operation Werewolf "Division" simply refers to a confederated group of three or more individuals in one geographical area who meet for training and other community endeavors. One of these individuals will be named Kommandant, President, or other title to denote his position as "head of operations." He will be the point of contact for the Division for any official communications.

All Divisions are expected to exhaustively research their area to determine if there are other Divisions already operating in their area and to handle this communication on their own, determining whether or not it would be better to simply attempt to join the existing one, or whether difference in practice and application call for the formation of their own Division.

At this time, in order to attain official recognition, a Division must attend either Baldr's Funeral or a Winter War event. The understanding of these terminologies and how to attend are left to the Division to learn and experience first-hand. There is a value in this sort of discovery and the immersion into the culture that it requires. All of these factors lend themselves toward an armor against the insincere, the tourist, and the interloper.

Each Division is encouraged to develop its own internal culture, symbols, rituals and style, but to represent Operation Werewolf is to understand that this is not a platform for a Division's personal politics, and that to exist within the framework of Operation Werewolf is to eschew or abandon the modern sickness of belief in a political solution at all.

Operation Werewolf is not nationalist, communist, anarchist, or fascist. It is a culture of strength, building tribes that value the honor code established previously--there is no hidden agenda, shadowy associations, nor underhanded mission. If we were any of these things, we would proudly and aggressively display it, as we have proudly and aggressively displayed other symbols and concepts that have led to

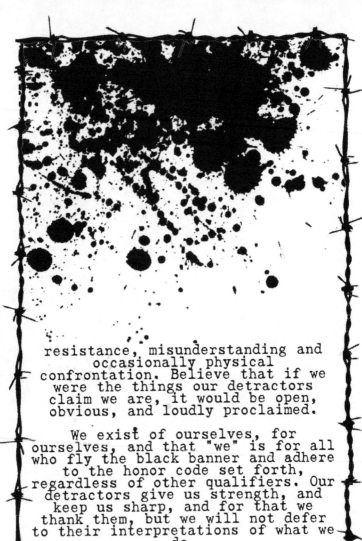

resistance, misunderstanding and
occasionally physical
confrontation. Believe that if we
were the things our detractors
claim we are, it would be open,
obvious, and loudly proclaimed.

We exist of ourselves, for
ourselves, and that "we" is for all
who fly the black banner and adhere
to the honor code set forth,
regardless of other qualifiers. Our
detractors give us strength, and
keep us sharp, and for that we
thank them, but we will not defer
to their interpretations of what we
do.

Public displays of political
affiliation and other philosophies
that are in direct conflict with
the internal core of Operation
Werewolf are a flagrant act of
dishonor and should be corrected by
those who are true to the nature of
what we seek to accomplish.

IRON FIST

The idea of the Iron Fist was
conceived in the earliest stages of
Operation Werewolf's development.
It was understood from the
beginning that this idea would take
time to come to fruition--this
level of patient, consistent
forward movement is something that
we stress in every area of
practice, and has been embedded in
the very nature of Operation
Werewolf's approach from its
inception.

In the operations manual of this
ongoing struggle, we are
on page 4 of 4,000.

Too often, organizations and confederations of people rush conceptual ideas toward manifestation, skipping important steps of germination, growth, direction, pruning, re-growth, and so on along the way. They are like someone who tries to bend a young tree toward where they want it to grow physically, straining hard against the untested limb until it snaps. This can be contrasted with the careful steward, who checks the soil, intently studies development, removes unnecessary "suckers" or twigs, eliminates dead branches, and creates an environment in which the young organism can thrive and have time to put roots down and stretch :S:unward.

Proper growth takes time, dedication, planning and patience. For a structure to support internal orders, it must first have a framework, along which slow, organic maturing can happen. It is only natural that the first internal order that has been announced is the Iron Fist- an elite brotherhood that will offer membership only to a select few who perform at the highest levels of the Operation in regard to physical prowess, dedication to martial training, travel, and self-reliance.

When its inception was announced, there were many people who assumed they would be automatically named, or offered a position in this order. They were wrong. The standards for consideration. what will be understood as the lowest standards acceptable, are not there to be bent at the beginning, prematurely corrupting something that will be, by its nature, a pure expression of strength and high accountability and performance.

Many people expressed disbelief that the standards for physicality, travel, and personal financial responsibility were unrealistically high. These individuals will more than likely never be considered for membership in their lifetime. Operation Werewolf is about setting high goals, mythic mountains to scale and undertake, trial and ordeal to be subjected to, and legends made. Unfortunately, many people who wrongfully associate themselves with us represent the exact opposite of these things. The Iron Fist will give those who distill the purest tenets of the Operation's devotion to both temporal and eternal power a niche of their own, a living temple made up of human beings who strive toward the highest goals.

That idea makes up the backbone, and the watchwords of the Iron Fist. Their words, *"Ad altiora tendo,"* translate from the Latin as, "I strive toward higher things." In June of 2018, at Baldr's Funeral, the first brothers of the Iron Fist will be named, and induction rituals performed.

The standards for consideration of membership into the Iron Fist are as follows:

Strength:

Overhead Press 1x bodyweight.
Bench Press 1.5x bodyweight
Squat 2x bodyweight
Deadlift 2.5x bodyweight

Train in a chosen martial art and compete.

Devotion:

Meet 3 Divisions by attending their individually hosted events.
Attend Winter War and/or Baldr's Funeral each year.
Travel to another country.

Temporal:

Start a business and put into the black (making profit).

MOVING
FORWARD

The style and arrangement of
Operation Werewolf is such that an
individual can align themselves
with its philosophies in a
deliberate, transformative way.
They are free to choose their own
level of involvement, remaining a
solitary practitioner or seeking
out division or living honor group.
From there, if they pay attention
and do the work, they may find
themselves invited to clandestine
gatherings of strength ritual and
tribal observances. This ongoing
narrative of Operation Werewolf is
a living and growing one,
strengthened and made holy by the
blood and deed of those who are
connected to it.

There may be those others who find themselves already in agreement with its beliefs and practices, and choose not to directly align, but to support at a distance and to direct others toward us who may find it valuable--we salute you also, as friends to our cause.

There is a hidden road inward, there for those who know where and how to look. This road is one of trial and ordeal, and involves total immersion into the lifestyle and becoming that Operation Werewolf represents. It is for the intrepid, the daring, the courageous, and those who seek to make their life a devotion to strength, loyalty and honor.

In reading this, many of you have taken the first step on that road, but it is littered on all sides with empty words, forgotten oaths, and hollow promises, as well as broken convictions, shattered wills and ruined intention.

If your footsteps don't falter, then every one of them will lead you to the center.
I'll see you out there.

XCII.
--P.W.

Paul Waggener is a founding member of the Wolves, a present day American tribe of men and women carving out a new mythology amongst the ruins of Empire. He is also the founder of Operation Werewolf, a program of Total Life Reform and aggressive self transformation. His written works can be found on Amazon as well as at the main Operation Werewolf website www.operationwerewolf.com

Made in United States
Troutdale, OR
09/25/2023

13174837R00039